How to Handle Stress the Easy way

A Step by Step Guide to Reducing and Managing Stress at Work

I0462914

By Meir Liraz

Published by BizMove
www.bizmove.com

Table of Contents

MEIR LIRAZ

1. Introduction

You need stress in your life! Does that surprise you? Perhaps so, but it is quite true. Without stress, life would be dull and unexciting. Stress adds flavor, challenge, and opportunity to life. Too much stress, however, can seriously affect your physical and mental well-being. A major challenge in this stress-filled world of today is to make the stress in your life work for you instead of against you.

Stress is with us all the time. It comes from mental or emotional activity and physical activity. It is unique and personal to each of us. So personal, in fact, that what may be relaxing to one person may be stressful to another. For example, if you're a busy executive who likes to keep busy all the time, "taking it easy" at the beach on a beautiful day may feel extremely frustrating, nonproductive, and upsetting. You may be emotionally distressed from "doing nothing."

Too much emotional stress can cause physical illness such as high blood pressure, ulcers, or even heart disease; physical stress from work or exercise is not likely to cause such ailments. The truth is that physical exercise can help you to relax and to handle your mental or emotional stress.

Hans Selye, M.D., a recognized expert in the field, has defined stress as a "non-specific response of the body to a demand." The important issue is learning how our bodies respond to these demands. When stress becomes prolonged or particularly frustrating, it can become harmful-causing distress or "bad stress." Recognizing the early signs of distress and then doing something about them can make an important difference in the quality of your life, and may actually influence your survival.

2. Reacting to Stress

To use stress in a positive way and prevent it from becoming distress, you should become aware of your own reactions to stressful events. The body responds to stress by going through three stages: (1) alarm, (2) resistance, and (3) exhaustion.

Let's take the example of a typical commuter in rush-hour traffic. If a car suddenly pulls out in front of him, his initial alarm reaction may include fear of an accident, anger at the driver who committed the action, and general frustration. His body may respond in the alarm stage by releasing hormones into the bloodstream which cause his face to flush, perspiration to form, his stomach to have a sinking feeling, and his arms and legs to tighten. The next stage is resistance, in which the body repairs damage caused by the stress. If the stress of driving continues with repeated close calls or traffic jams, however, his body will not have time to make repairs. He may become so conditioned to expect potential problems when he drives that he tightens up at the beginning of each commuting day. Eventually, he may even develop one of the diseases of stress, such as migraine headaches, high blood pressure, backaches, or insomnia. While it is impossible to live completely free of stress and distress, it is possible to prevent some distress as well as to minimize its impact when it can't be avoided.

3. Helping Yourself

When stress does occur, it is important to recognize and deal with it. Here are some suggestions for ways to handle stress. As you begin to understand more about how stress affects you as an individual, you will come up with your own ideas of helping to ease the tensions.

Try physical activity. When you are nervous, angry, or upset, release the pressure through exercise or physical activity. Running, walking, playing tennis, or working in your garden are just some of the activities you might try. Physical exercise will relieve that "up tight" feeling, relax you, and turn the frowns into smiles. Remember, your body and your mind work together.

Share your stress. It helps to talk to someone about your concerns and worries. Perhaps a friend, family member, teacher, or counselor can help you see your problem in a different light. If you feel your problem is serious, you might seek professional help from a psychologist, psychiatrist, or social worker. Knowing when to ask for help may avoid more serious problems later.

Know your limits. If a problem is beyond your

control and cannot be changed at the moment, don't fight the situation. Learn to accept what is-for now-until such time when you can change it.

Take care of yourself. You are special. Get enough rest and eat well. If you are irritable and tense from lack of sleep or if you are not eating correctly, you will have less ability to deal with stressful situations. If stress repeatedly keeps you from sleeping, you should ask your doctor for help.

Make time for fun. Schedule time for both work and recreation. Play can be just as important to your well-being as work; you need a break from your daily routine to just relax and have fun.

Be a participant. One way to keep from getting bored, sad, and lonely is to go where it's all happening: Sitting alone can make you feel frustrated. Instead of feeling sorry for yourself, get involved and become a participant. Offer your services in neighborhood or volunteer organizations. Help yourself by helping other people. Get involved in the world and the people around you, and you'll find they will be attracted to you. You're on your way to making new friends and enjoying new activities.

Check off your tasks. Trying to take care of everything at once can seem overwhelming, and, as a result, you may not accomplish anything, Instead, make a list of what tasks you have to do, then do one at a time, checking them off as they're completed. Give priority to the most important ones and do those first.

Must you always be right? Do other people upset you - particularly when they don't do things your way? Try cooperation instead of confrontation; it's better than fighting and always being "right:" A little give and take on both sides will reduce the strain and make you both feel more comfortable.

It's OK to cry. A good cry can be a healthy way to bring relief to your anxiety, and it might even prevent a headache or other physical consequence. Take some deep breaths; they also release tension.

Create a quiet scene. You can't always run away, but you can "dream the impossible dream." A quiet country scene painted mentally, or on canvas, can take you out of the turmoil of a stressful situation. Change the scene by reading a good book or playing beautiful music to create a sense of peace and tranquillity.

Avoid self-medication. Although you can use drugs to relieve stress temporarily, drugs do not remove the conditions that caused the stress in the first place. Drugs, in fact, may be habit-forming and create more stress than they take away. They should be taken :only on the advice of your doctor.

4. The Art of Relaxation

The best strategy for avoiding stress is to learn how to relax. Unfortunately, many people try to relax at the same pace that they lead the rest of their lives. For a while, tune out your worries about time, productivity, and "doing right." You will find satisfaction in just being, without striving. Find activities that give you pleasure and that are good for your mental and physical well-being. Forget about always winning. Focus on relaxation, enjoyment, and health. Be good to yourself.

5. How to Overcome Fear and Anxiety

When faced with fear, we often talk ourselves out of taking action. Most of the time, we have nothing to lose and everything to gain!

1. Breathe!

When we are excited, we get body sensations that can stop us. Stop, take some deep breaths and then proceed. This is especially important to help your voice sound calm when your knees are shaking.

2. Remember, it isn't about you!

When you get rejection, it is usually because the other person doesn't need what you are offering. It isn't personal. They may just be having a bad day. Or if they are genuinely a nasty person, they gave you a break by not prolonging the relationship!

3. Picture The WORST

Can you live through that? We awfulize most things and imagine the outcome far worse than it usually is. Ask yourself, what is the worst that can happen? Most of the time, you can handle it!

4. **Master The Topic**

If we feel confident in our knowledge, the fear about sharing it with others decreases. Even if they don't see value or agree with us, we feel okay, because we have developed an expertise that gives us confidence in ourselves.

5. **Put something at stake or give yourself reward**

A reward or penalty that is big enough will motivate sometimes. A sales trainer coached a real estate agent in making regular prospecting calls to write a check for $1000 to his ex-wife and have his secretary send it any day he did not make the number of prospecting calls he said he would.

6. **Get a Buddy**

Taking on something fearful with another person often will get you through it and keep you from having those dialogues in your head that try to talk you out of it. A coach can also help shine light into those dark areas!

7. **Talk about it out loud**

Once you identify the fear and talk about it out

loud, it will often diminish. Another technique is to close your eyes and picture yourself doing that thing you are afraid to do. Now run through the same scene but do it very fast. Now run through it very slow, next make it silly, make it brighter, make it dimmer. Has some of the fear dissipated?

8. Read something inspirational or listen to tapes.

Play your favorite motivational tape or read something inspirational right before you take action to help your mind focus on what is POSSIBLE rather than what could derail you. Think about how you will feel when you have taken action. Write down the top 10 feelings you'll have when you have done this thing!

9. Use your strengths-take the easy way!

Sometimes we focus on thinking we "should" do things that just aren't our strengths. Take a look to see if you can accomplish what you want some other way. What easy ones can you do first? How can you leverage what you already have without having to tackle an unknown.

10. If you have a frog to swallow, do it quickly

Don't look at it too long. Sometimes, there is no way around the fact, you are going to have to take an action that is fearful. The longer you fret about it, there more energy you waste. JUST DO IT!!!!

6. How to Be Empowered

Contrary to common belief, the most effective control over one's life can be gained in an almost effortless manner. The truly empowered person "has it together", exudes a glowing poise that is apparent to others. Here are ten steps whereby you can begin experience empowerment in your own life.

1. **Start from where you are and take one step at a time.**

When you think about it, that's the only place you CAN start, i.e., where you are at this moment. Begin with your present perceptions, understandings, and strengths and move forward, one step at a time. In this world of objectives, goals and big plans, we often focus too much on the future with the result that our ability to concentrate fully on the present is severely compromised. Yet, it is only in the present that we can make a difference.

2. **Examine your resistance points--the things that irritate you, limit you, or cause you to react.**

We often resist what we most need to learn. The

next time you find yourself resisting new information, a particular situation, or something someone else is saying, ask yourself: What is it that is really bothering me about this? Is there something that I need to learn?

3. **Recognize that whatever you are experiencing at this very moment is appropriate to your need to grow.**

Implicit in this "rule of appropriateness" is the concept that there is a larger plan of which you are an integral part. Until you're willing to acknowledge the possibility that such a plan exists, you will never be able to see it!

4. **Stop worrying about whether others are getting theirs!**

It's easy to become preoccupied about what the other person is doing, getting, achieving, etc. This kind of worrying is useless and wastes time and energies that are better spent on yourself.

5. **Realize that it doesn't matter what happened to you or who did it to you; the only thing that matters is what you do about it.**

What happened and who did it to you are in the

past. You can't change the past, you can only change your perception of it. The ONLY thing that counts is what you do NOW in order to move forward.

6. Learn to withhold judgment.

To withhold judgment is to accept what is. How often in conversation do you find yourself mentally correcting, criticizing, or re-phrasing? when you do, you risk missing the real message which may not be in the words themselves. Rather than saying to yourself, "that's inaccurate" or "he/she is wrong", try accepting the statement as simply a representation of the way that person thinks, feels or what he/she intends to convey. This simple technique can open up a whole realm of hidden meaning, AND it enables you to respond more objectively and dispassionately.

7. Learn to operate holistically by opening up to the other possibilities that are always there.

There is always more than one way to solve a problem. You're most likely to get "stuck" when you foreclose your options by setting up conditions, demands, expectations, fears, positions and prejudices.

8. **Complete your unfinished business.**

Most of us have "unfinished business"--failures, a relationship gone sour, or a good deed left undone. Getting beyond ("completing") is not always easy, but there's a three-step process that, if followed, can do wonders for your psyche. It's this: (1) Acknowledge the wrong, mistake, screw-up, etc. to yourself, (2) Admit it to one other person, preferably the person you've wronged and, in the latter case, apologize and ask simply: "What can I do to make this right with you?" (Sometimes there really isn't much you can do, but the simple act of asking is healing in itself), and (3) Move ON. You've admitted your mistake, taken whatever corrective action you could, and now it's time to go forward. This third step takes discipline, but it works.

9. **When faced with an apparently hopeless situation, take action, any action.**

There's something called the "logjam" theory that applies here: when logs in a stream become all jammed up, moving ANY ONE log frees the others to move, because the act of moving a single piece creates space which in turn allows the other pieces to move. It's important to recognize that you're not trying to reach a final solution in a single move; you're simply taking "one step at a time" (Step#1)

10. Consider the wisdom of doing absolutely nothing!

As with the rule of appropriateness (above), there's a hidden assumption here, namely, that we each possess an inner wisdom that is always available if we know how to tap into it. Call it intuition, spiritual sense, whatever, the fact is that this "still small voice" is audible only when we are very quiet. It's a bit like a point in which you can see the bottom only when the surface is calm and the water nu-muddied. Doing nothing means exactly that: nothing physically, nothing mentally, nothing at all! The Japanese call it, "kokoro-no-mizu", literally, a "mind as water"--smooth, flowing and undisturbed. Try it. It works, and it's fun!

www.ingramcontent.com/pod-product-compliance
Lightning Source LLC
Chambersburg PA
CBHW072312170526
45158CB00003BA/1287